AUSTRALIA
Land of Wonder

AUSTRALIA
Land of Wonder

Alan Johnson

CURREY O'NEIL

Land of Wonder.

Left: The ghost gum, Eucalyptus papuana, *of northern and central Australia, has become to many Australians a symbol of the inland. It began to attract particular interest about thirty years ago through the works of the Aboriginal artist Albert Namatjira, and ghost gum paintings by Namatjira's fellow Arunta tribesmen are still sought today by tourists in the Northern Territory. This striking tree is also an outstanding subject for photographers, and must vie with the great river red gums as the most photographed of all Australia's native trees. The smooth pale bark of the tree is made more vivid by the presence of a fine powdery dust which is almost white. The outer layer of bark is shed as the tree grows and there is sometimes a band of old bark pieces extending a short distance up from the base of the tree. The ghost gum ranges in height from nine to twenty metres and the foliage has a characteristic drooping appearance. This magnificent species is growing near Trephina Gorge in the Northern Territory.*

The very face of this ancient continent is a thing of wonder. It is the flattest of all the world's great land masses. Only one twenty-fifth of Australia's land surface rises to more than 600 metres above sea level (the average elevation for the world is 700 metres) and in fact the *average* land height is just half of that. A look at the map of Australia will quickly show that the only region which might be called mountainous is the narrow strip of highlands along the eastern coastline. The paucity of highlands and the concentration of what there are on one edge of the continent means that Australia is also the driest of the inhabited continents; only Antarctica receives less rainfall. Roughly forty per cent of Australia is classified as desert.

Despite this sobering fact, the range of vegetation and natural landscapes is surprisingly wide. The dry areas of Australia are very dry and the wet areas very wet. In the inland it is quite common for substantial river systems flowing westward towards the centre to simply disappear into nothing: to spread out into numerous branchlets which in turn become chains of waterholes and ultimately evaporate or soak away. Australia's largest lake, Lake Eyre in South Australia, exists only intermittently. For most of the time its 9 000 square-kilometre bed is dry land or salt pan. It seldom fills to anything resembling its official size. The last major filling was in 1974 and the most important before that in 1951. More than seventy-five per cent of the continent experiences a rate of evaporation higher than the rainfall; half the continent has an evaporation rate *double* the rainfall rate. The total run-off of all Australian rivers is less than one-tenth that of the Amazon. In spite of this, Australia's water resources are quite substantial in relationship to its comparatively small population. In many areas supply exceeds need and water runs to waste. Australia's wettest town – Tully, in Queensland – has a rainfall of four-and-a-half metres every year.

Only in the east, where the Great Dividing Range curves like a submerged backbone from Cape York in the north to south-eastern Victoria, are there mountains worthy of the name. On these highlands most of the rain falls, and where the rain falls the forests grow. The dominant tree of the east – and indeed of the continent – is the *Eucalyptus* or 'gum tree'. This genus of myrtle contains more than 500 species and accounts for ninety-five per cent of the forests. The variety of the eucalypts – and the other major tree group, the acacias – is enormous. Encompassing well over one thousand species between them, these trees range from forest giants to the low, straggly mallees which thrive in arid regions and grow to no more than a few metres high. Many of Australia's native animals and birds live in close association with these two tree groups; they feed on the flowers, fruits, leaves, or buds, or upon the insects found near them.

The fauna of Australia has been shaped to a degree by isolation. The continent has been separated from any other land mass for a least sixty million years, a fact which has had two important consequences. Firstly, it has allowed some of Nature's most primitive creatures to survive in Australia long after they disappeared from other regions of the world. Secondly, it has enabled significant groups of animals, such as the marsupials, to flourish and extend with little interference, protected from migratory predators or excessive competition between the species. The characteristics of the native fauna have also been influenced by the need to adapt to the environment. Australia has few extensive areas of grazing land rich enough to support herds of large animals like buffaloes or deer. Instead, adaptation to dry conditions is a notable feature of nearly all categories of the native fauna. Large meat-eaters like the northern hemisphere bears or lions and other big cats of Africa, are absent; the Australian fauna is largely herbivorous, feeding on grasses or the leaves, seeds and flowers of native vegetation. The breeding activity of many birds is associated with, or subject to, rainfall; fewer young are reared in dry seasons than when the rains have been good. Most native mammals, reptiles and birds have the ability to go for long periods without water; some never drink, obtaining the moisture they need from their diet.

The Australian fauna is notable in that it contains important groups of animals which are either sparsely represented or not found at all in other regions of the world. Here, too, we find groups of animals which, through their isolation, have developed quite differently over millions of years from their biological relatives in the northern hemisphere. The monotremes are an example of the former category.

Their sole representatives, the platypus and echidna, are the last survivors of an ancient and primitive class of animals. The female platypus and echidna lay eggs in the manner of reptiles and birds but after incubation and hatching, suckle their young in the mammalian fashion. Some scientists regard the ancestors of the monotremes as a stage in the evolution of mammals from reptiles.

The other important group among the native fauna contains the marsupials, and includes such well-known animals as the kangaroos and possums, the wombat and the koala. Marsupials are distinguished from the other mammals by the fact that the young are not fully formed at birth. Instead the offspring are born in a semi-developed state and complete their early development in a pouch (marsupium) which has an opening on the external surface of the female's body and serves as a kind of substitute womb. The young of the red kangaroo, for instance, is scarcely larger than a bean when it is born.

The bird life of Australia is abundant; in proportion to area there are twice as many species as in North America and there is more variety among the birds than almost any other group of native fauna. Since the movements of birds are not restricted in the same way as ground-dwelling creatures, the isolation of the continent has not had the influence on Australia's avifauna that it has had on its mammals. There is considerable 'overlap' between species found here and in the northern islands and southern Asia. Roughly 750 species of birds are found in the continent, plus introduced species and migrants such as seabirds. Of this number about 500 are land-dwelling birds, and some 350 of these belong to the order of passerines or perching song-birds. In this order we find almost seventy species of honeyeaters and many small, colourful songsters such as robins, fantails, flycatchers, finches and wrens, together with the larger magpies and butcher birds. Here, too, are individual species of particular interest: the bower birds which, in addition to their nests, build tunnel- or tent-like structures of sticks and grass decorated with pieces of glass, shells and other colourful objects – and the lyrebird, which spreads its lacy tail like a fan to perform the most exquisite dances, and can mimic innumerable bird calls and forest sounds. Among the other bird groups are the flightless emu, which can weigh up to sixty-eight kilograms, and about fifty species of native parrots one group of which, the screeching, crested cockatoos, is found only in this region.

In one outstanding region of Australia the wonders of the physical world and of the animal world can be seen combined in what is, without question, one of nature's great marvels: the Great Barrier Reef. This vast agglomeration of coral reefs and islands lies just off the north-eastern coast of Queensland and extends for roughly 2 000 kilometres from just north of Brisbane to the island of New Guinea. The Great Barrier Reef is the product of the tiny coral animal and is often cited as the largest construction made by living creatures, though it is important to note that 'the reef' is not a single structure but rather a collection of natural formations. The coral animal or polyp is a relative of the sea anemone but differs from it in two important respects. First, the adult animal has no means of propulsion; second, it has the ability to extract calcium from the sea water. The body of the coral animal is divided into a number of sections by flat vertical tissues and the calcium absorbed from the water is deposited along these sections and on the base of the animal so that eventually it becomes enclosed of a stony cup of its own making. When the living creature dies the cups remain embedded in the calcareous lump the coral animals have formed. Most coral polyps are only about the size of a pin's head and the rate at which they deposit calcium is very slow. Studies made on the Great Barrier Reef indicate that some of the corals there have grown at the rate of 49 metres in 1 000 years. Over the centuries the reefs built up by the corals have spread over 207 000 square kilometres.

In the warm tropical waters of the reef area many molluscs grow to uncommon size. The bailer shell, which was once used by the native tribes of the north to bail their canoes, grows to 46 centimetres long and contains a living animal which may weigh more than a kilogram. The giant clam, largest of the world's molluscs, can weigh more than 226 kilograms but despite its formidable appearance is not, as legend suggests, in the habit of snapping closed on the legs of unwary divers. Not all the shells of the reefs, however, are harmless. Many are flesh-eaters, preying on other living molluscs and sea creatures. Some are poisonous, like the cone shells, which first sting their victims then rasp away their flesh with their abrasive ribbon tongue.

The reef is home for a myriad of diverse creatures, and yet they represent only a small number of natural wonders which may be seen and experienced in Australia. That so many of these have survived virtually untouched since prehistoric times for us to marvel at today is perhaps the greatest wonder of all.

Despite the rapid and continuing development of its mining and manufacturing industries, Australia remains an important agricultural and livestock-producing nation. The growth of secondary industry has lessened the country's dependence on exports of wheat, wool and meat but these are still significant. The stockman, the drover and the shearer are still a part of everyday life in much of rural Australia. Like his nineteenth-century counterpart, today's drover will still, most likely, be mounted on horseback, and his only companions for perhaps days on end will be a pair of trusted working dogs. The photograph at left was taken in the cattle country of the Dorrigo Plateau in the New England area of New South Wales. The dogs are Border Collie-Kelpie crosses: hardy, loyal and intelligent dogs which work alongside men as respected companions. Decades of breeding have produced today's cattle- and sheep-dogs and the best of them are highly prized.

Below: Sheep on the road at Kangaroo Gap near Rawley's Bluff in the Flinders Ranges, South Australia.

Shearing time is the busiest of all on an Australian sheep station. It's a time when everyone works tirelessly. The day starts at sun-up and ends only when the last rays of light flicker on the evening horizon. Once again, the working dogs are an essential part of the scene. A good sheep-dog uses plenty of 'eye' to control the mob, half-crouching as he moves cautiously, watching the sheep intently as if mesmerising them. His sense of balance is superb, his brain is working like a computer. He is oblivious to all around him. The Kelpie (below, left) is one of the most popular breeds. The man on the land well knows the importance of his working dogs: they will handle the most difficult jobs set before them in drought or flood, hot weather or cold. Emu Bottom (right) is a restored historic homestead near Sunbury, Victoria. It was established by a pioneer, George Evans, in 1835 and its shearing shed of roughly-hewn timbers is characteristic of the style which prevailed in succeeding decades.

Over page: Sunset in the Australian outback. The long working day is over, and as darkness falls some weary horsemen bring a mob of wild horses into the yards.

The Australian continent – which extends for more than 3 000 kilometres from north to south and approximately 4 000 kilometres from west to east – has a coastline of some 20 000 kilometres. Encompassing a land mass of such size, it is consequently a coastline of enormous variety. The continent is bordered by three great oceans: the Indian on the west, the Pacific on the east and the Southern, which stretches to the Antarctic. A majority of Australians live within easy travelling distance of the Pacific – as its name suggests, one of the world's more peaceful seas. It is Australia's gateway to the world and a prime source of recreation, with beaches, surf and expanses ideal for 'blue-water' yachting. Along the eastern seaboard the coast is pitted with hundreds of safe harbours for small craft. Lord Howe Island (below) is one of the large islands in the Pacific off the east coast. Its striking terrain is typified by the massive bulk of Mts Lidgbird and Gower.

Right: Peaceful coastline near Boat Harbour in north-west Tasmania, looking towards Rocky Cape.

Along Australia's southern coastline, under the influence of the 'roaring forties', the prevailing weather comes from the strong westerly winds which funnel through Bass Strait. Windand waves constantly assail the coastline, slowly but surely eroding the tall rocky cliffs that mark the edge of the continent. Weathering has produced some unusual rock formations along the southern coasts but the most significant of these must be the towering cliffs of the Great Australian Bight. Here, along parts of the Nullarbor Plain, the surface of the land is more than ninety metres above the water.

Left: Tasman Arch, one of several remarkable rock formations on the Tasman Peninsula in south-east Tasmania. Right: Waves breaking on the rocky Pacific coast, southern New South Wales. Below: The southern edge of the Nullarbor Plain ends abruptly in the sheer cliffs of the Great Australian Bight, South Australia.

Some of the most dramatic coastal scenery in Australia occurs on the southern tip of the Tasman Peninsula (right). This rugged area is linked to the Tasmanian mainland – via Forestier Peninsula – by slender bridges of land. Its remoteness from the early settlements and the inhospitable character of much of its coastline were among the reasons it was chosen to be a penal settlement in the convict days of last century. At nearby Port Arthur thousands of convicts were housed in a penitentiary, and Eaglehawk Neck, the isthmus which joins the two peninsulas, was guarded by lookouts and a tethered chain of fierce dogs. Tasman Island (right) which looks across a narrow strait to the towering rocky cliffs of Cape Pillar, lies off the southernmost point of the peninsula.

Over page: Of striking contrast are the warm and tranquil waters of Shute Harbour on the central Queensland coast. The harbour, which lies within the Mount Conway National Park, opens on to the waters of the Whitsunday Passage, one of Queensland's most favoured tourist areas. Beyond are the coral-studded waters of the Great Barrier Reef.

Australia, with few major mountain ranges, is one of the world's drier continents. A large part of the land surface is technically desert, and in almost all areas water is at a premium. In eastern Australia most of the river systems are associated with the Great Dividing Range. Rivers which flow to the east are generally short and vigorous; those which flow to the west often spread out over thousands of kilometres of the inland plains. The major western rivers – the Darling, the Murrumbidgee and the Murray – nourish and irrigate much of pastoral Australia. The Murray is perhaps the most famous of these. Rising in southern New South Wales, it flows westwards, forming the boundary between New South Wales and Victoria. After crossing the South Australian border it turns to the south and spills across its flood plain to Lake Alexandrina and the Southern Ocean. At many points its progress is slowed by water storages such as Lake Hume (below) near Albury but always its course is marked by Murray River red gums (left).

Above: River red gums at the edge of a lake in the Wyperfeld National Park in north-eastern Victoria.

Many of the capital cities of the Australian States are built on the banks of a river. Perhaps the most beautiful of these city sites is that of Hobart, capital of Tasmania, which overlooks the broad estuary of the Derwent River. The harbour here is one of the world's finest, accessible at any tide to the largest vessels. In the early days, it was a haven for whalers and sealers, and it has seen the departure of many expeditions to the Antarctic. Today the ocean-going yachts of the celebrated Sydney-to-Hobart race sail up the Derwent at the end of the race to moorings in Hobart's Constitution Dock. Not far away is sheltered Sandy Bay (above) whose waters reflect the tower of the Wrest Point casino. Melbourne is another river city. The Yarra River (below) flows through bushland in its upper reaches and at its mouth forms the main port for Victoria.

Right: Sunset at Pitt Water, an inlet of Broken Bay at the mouth of the Hawkesbury River north of Sydney. Over page: Black swans on Lake Wendouree at Ballarat, Victoria.

Australia has a rich variety of native trees and flowers. The trees are dominated by two large groups: the acacias, commonly called 'wattles', of which there are approximately 600 species – and the eucalypts, commonly called 'gum trees', of which there are about 500. Wattles vary from small shrubs to tall trees. Their distinguishing feature (left) is the flower – a small powderpuff made by the stamens, usually golden in colour but in some species yellow and, occasionally, white. The popularity of wattles is reflected in the wealth of common names bestowed on them: golden wattle, silver wattle, mulga, myall, boree, brigalow, dead-finish and gidgee are but a few. Some species are called prickly moses, from the word 'mimosa' – the English name for an acacia. 'Wattle' is an old English word for a structure made by intertwining pliable saplings. Using such wattles plastered with mud, buildings could easily be made, and the early settlers transferred the name to the trees that provided these stems.

Eucalypts came to be called 'gum trees' because of the habit of some species of exuding a gum-like substance from wounds on the trunk: they are not related to the trees which produce true gum. Among the eucalypts may be found the world's tallest flowering trees. The mountain ash, *Eucalyptus regnans*, can grow to more than 100 metres. The tallest living specimen is growing in Tasmania and has reached ninety-nine metres. Eucalypts have unique and appealing – though often subtle – flowers. The flowers at top right are those of the mottlecah, a Western Australian species, and are the largest of any eucalypt, measuring up to 75 mm in diameter. The scarlet-flowering gum (below right) is another tree from Western Australia but is widely cultivated elsewhere for its brilliant floral display in mid-summer.

The word eucalypt means 'well-covered' and is a reference to the tightly-fitting cap which seals the flower-bud before it opens. Eucalypt flowers have no petals or sepals; the beauty of the flower comes from the filaments which, as the bud develops, push off the cap. The colour of the flower is also a signal to many native birds and nocturnal mammals (such as possums) which feed on nectar contained in the flower cup. The buds – which, when they have become dry and woody are often called 'gum nuts' – vary greatly in shape and size. Left: Long-flowered marlock, *Eucalyptus macrandra*. Below, left: Darwin woolybutt, *Eucalyptus miniata*. Below: Gungurru, *Eucalyptus caesia*.

Right: The mountain ash, *Eucalyptus regnans*, is a tree of the wet mountain forests of eastern Victoria and parts of Tasmania. These majestic eucalypts are the tallest hardwood trees in the world. There are several eucalypts in the Australian 'ash' group but they are not related to the European ash.

The Australian landscape painter Arthur Streeton once said that the colours of Australia were blue and gold. They are certainly colours which may be seen often during any summer in the Australian bush. The ground mistletoe or Christmas tree (right) of Western Australia is one of the most striking trees of the world when in flower. It begins life as a parasite, but instead of growing in the usual mistletoe fashion on the branches of a host tree, it fastens on to the roots (perhaps even of grasses) of nearby hosts. In early summer the blossoms of mature trees smother the leaves and branches in a blaze of gold. Gold and yellow are also colours associated with the many species of acacias. The elegant wattle, *Acacia victoriae* (below, left), is a small tree which grows to about four metres high. It is found mainly in inland South Australia, New South Wales, the Northern Territory and Queensland.

Above, left: Open eucalypt forest carpeted with wildflowers in Victoria.

Western Australia's tallest tree is *Eucalyptus diversicolor*, commonly known by its Aboriginal name, karri. Heights of around eighty metres have been recorded but karris of this size are no longer common. Like most of the other very tall eucalypts, the diameter of the tree is not very great in proportion to its height: the normal diameter of a very tall tree would be two or three metres. The greatest heights are reached when the trees are growing together in forests, competing for the available light. In these circumstances the trunks are very straight and smooth and the first branches do not appear until about one-third of the total height. 'Karri country' surrounds the town of Pemberton, about 300 kilometres south of Perth, and karri flourishes between Manjimup and Albany, where some of the world's finest hardwood forests may be seen. The culling of trees in these areas is strictly regulated. Within forests some of the best trees have been set aside as 'mother trees' to provide seed for new growth in the surrounding cleared areas. Many hundreds of thousands of hectares of karri forest have been declared national parks, but the protection of these magnificent eucalypts remains an active conservation issue.

The wildlife of Australia is rich and varied; it also contains many species of animals and birds quite unlike those found in the other continents. The most striking feature of the native mammals (there are more than 200 of them) is that almost half are marsupials – animals in which the young are born in an undeveloped state and complete their early growth in a breeding pouch with an external opening. The best-known of the marsupials is undoubtedly the kangaroo (right) which can move at great speed in hopping bounds, maintaining perfect balance with the help of a long powerful tail. Over short distances, large kangaroos can travel at forty kilometres-an-hour, and clear obstacles of nine metres. The young kangaroos, commonly called joeys, live in a pouch on the mother's belly until they are old enough to fend for themselves. The kangaroo family also includes the smaller wallaroos and wallabies. Large kangaroos stand about two metres high but the smallest members of the group are not much larger than large rats. Australia's other famous marsupial mammal is the koala (right, below), sometimes incorrectly called the 'native bear'. It is not related to the European bears and indeed its closest relative is thought to be the Australian wombat. Kangaroos are grazing animals of the plains and the koalas are leaf-eaters whose diet is provided by several species of eucalypts. Australia has no native hoofed animals, no large carnivores like lions and tigers, and no primates. The dingo (left) has long been regarded as Australia's native dog but its similarity to the domestic dog has caused scientists to speculate that it probably evolved from a domesticated or semi domesticated version of the Asiatic wolf and found its way to Australia in prehistoric times when the continent was joined by a land bridge to southern Asia. The dingo is generally limited to the arid inland areas of Australia, though there have been many recent claims that the animals can be domesticated. Dingoes, or Warrigals as they are also called, are predators, hunting mainly rabbits, small marsupials and ground-dwelling birds; they will also attack domestic stock and poultry.

There are more than 500 species of birds native to Australia. Most of them are wholly or partly insect-eaters, and in their native state feed in or around the eucalypts and wattles which dominate the native vegetation. The parrots are one of the world bird groups which are strongly represented in this continent. There are more than sixty Australian parrot species, including a number of the spectacular cockatoos and galahs. The pink-breasted galah (left) is one of the most appealing and best-known of these. Fortunately, in the eyes of bird-lovers, it is also one of the native species which seems to have benefited from man's disturbance of the environment; it is now probably more common than it ever was. The many waterholes and dams built for grazing and agriculture have helped the birds survive and flourish. The kingfisher family has a distinctive Australian representative in the laughing kookaburra (right). Its name is a reference to its call, perhaps the most distinctive of that given by any Australian bird. The 'laugh', however, has nothing to do with good humour. It is a call given to denote that an individual bird is within its own territory – into which other kookaburras may venture only at their peril. Largest of the Australian bird species is the flightless emu (below right), one of the great 'hikers' of the bird world. Some marked specimens have covered more than 500 kilometres between the time they were marked and the time they were recovered. The emu stands as high as a man: after the ostrich it is the largest bird in the world. Its legs are powerful and it is a fast runner. Emus timed from a moving car have reached, and been able to maintain, speeds of almost fifty kilometres an hour. Even when walking, the emu takes long (almost three metres) strides.

Perhaps the most remarkable region of the Australian continent is the arid interior. And the most remarkable part of the interior is the area commonly called Central Australia but known also as The Dead Heart or The Red Centre. Here is a landscape like no other on earth.

Glowing fiery red in the late afternoon light, Ayers Rock, in the Northern Territory, looms over the surrounding plains like a misshapen sun about to slip beneath the horizon. This is the greatest piece of exposed rock on the earth's surface, almost 350 metres high and more than eight kilometres around its circumference. Changing colour constantly throughout the day to mirror the prevailing light, it is, when seen from nearby, an astonishing and unique sight, rising abruptly from the surrounding plain of sand, spinifex grass and mulga. To the Aboriginal tribes of the region it is a sacred place, and the caves around its base contain priceless examples of their art. The rock was sighted in 1873 by the explorer William Gosse, who named it after Sir Henry Ayers, then governor of South Australia. Despite its remoteness from the capital cities – it stands 300 kilometres south-west of Alice Springs – it is, not surprisingly, one of the greatest single tourist attractions in Australia.

Only about thirty kilometres from Ayers Rock are the equally mysterious Olgas, a jumble of twenty-eight massive domed boulders. The Aboriginals of the area called the formation 'Katajuta', which means 'many heads'. The Olgas are as dramatic and as vividly coloured as Ayers Rock, lacking only the majesty of the Rock's great bulk. The tallest of the group, Mount Olga, is 546 metres above the oasis-like 'valley of the winds' that runs through the rock system. The explorer Ernest Giles, who first saw Mount Olga and named it after the Queen of Spain, described the rocks as 'minarets, giant cupolas and monstrous domes . . . huge memorials of the ancient times to the earth'.

The baobab trees of north-west Australia are another of nature's mysteries awaiting travellers in the continent's remote regions. These are among the most strangely-shaped trees in the world. The huge base, which may have a girth of ten metres, supports a number of apparently contorted branches. During the dry season the tree sheds all its leaves but with the arrival of the 'wet' it is clothed in green again. The trunks of baobabs are often hollow and thus act as water tanks. In pioneering days some trees were provided with jam tins on strings so that thirsty travellers could get water. One baobab near Wyndham, Western Australia, with a huge hollow trunk, was reputed to have been used as a natural prison cell. The same claim is made for the great tree (right) growing a few kilometres from Derby on King Sound in north-west Western Australia.

Another strikingly-coloured landform of inland Australia is the tangled mass of the MacDonnell Ranges in the Northern Territory, shown here from the air, with the peak of Mount Conway in the foreground. The MacDonnell ranges stretch for 480 kilometres across the southern part of the Northern Territory. In their midst, accessible only through Heavitree Gap Pass, nestles the town of Alice Springs. This best-known of central Australian settlements grew from a camp set up during the construction of the Overland Telegraph which crossed the ranges in 1872. The MacDonnells are noted for their brilliant and constantly-changing colours, a phenomenon caused by the reflection of the bright sun from the mica and sandstone of the ranges.

Dotted throughout the MacDonnell Ranges in the Northern Territory are examples of some of the most spectacular terrain in the nation's centre. Many of these features take the form of gaps or gorges carved over the centuries by rivers flowing through the MacDonnells. Several of these gorges – Ormiston, Glen Helen (above) and Serpentine (left) – are situated on streams which are tributaries of the Finke River. The Finke River is one of the oldest watercourses in the world, and to walk along its bed, with the red walls towering above, is a memorable experience. Glen Helen tourist camp, about 130 kilometres west of Alice Springs, is a base for trips to explore the region. Finke River Gorge, further south, has amazing rock formations, while nearby Palm Valley provides a sudden contrast, with beautiful rock pools and ancient cycad and Livistona palms. Some of the palms growing here are relics of ancient times when Australia had a wetter climate and similar palms were spread over much of the continent.

A world away from the heat and vibrant primary colours of the arid inland is the silent frozen landscape of the Australian Antarctic Territory. Australia's relationship with Antarctica dates back to prehistoric times when the two continents were one, and it is fitting that Australia participated in the early exploration of this vast icy land. In 1954 the first permanent Australian base on the continent was established at Mawson for survey and scientific research programmes. Situated 5 840 kilometres south of Melbourne on the east coast of Mac.Robertson Land, Mawson is one of the windiest places on earth, experiencing an average wind velocity of twenty-one knots over a full year and with speeds of up to 114 knots recorded. Temperatures range from about five degrees celsius in summer to minus thirty-three degrees celsius in late winter and early spring. The nearest human habitation is at Davis base, 634 kilometres to the east, and during the dark Antarctic winter Mawson is inaccessible. Life at the base is busy but isolated and perhaps this is one reason why its inhabitants take a special interest in the progress and welfare of the thirty or so resident huskies. These animals are used to pull sleds and are among the toughest and most rugged of all dogs. The team at right is setting out on a twenty-four

kilometre Sunday afternoon photographic expedition to a grounded iceberg nine kilometres from the coast. Conditions are sparkling and sunny, for it is late spring and the temperature on the sea ice is a relatively warm minus six degrees. Antarctic conditions are not always as kind as this.

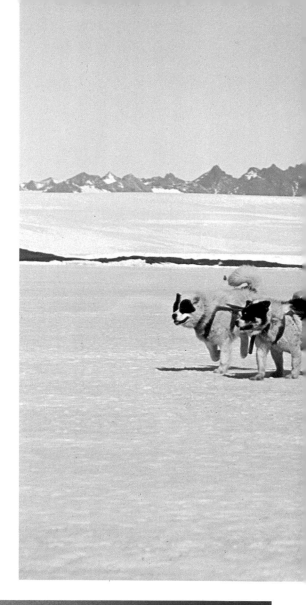

On the eastern coast of Australia, north of the Tropic of Capricorn, may be found the warm wet landscapes of tropical Australia. The spectacular waterfall (above) at Wallaman Falls National Park, north-eastern Queensland, plummets 300 metres to be dispersed on rocks in the rainforest below.

The Pinnacle (right) is the name given to the towering peak that majestically rises above the palms in the Cape Hillsborough National Park. The park, forty-five kiometres north of Mckay and overlooking the Hillsborough Channel off Queensland's central coast, is a montage of rugged seashores, caves and hills. Camping, swimming, bushwalking and fishing are among the available recreations.

The tropical rainforest of northern Australia is the most luxuriant of all plant worlds; it is forest pled on forest. The canopy or ceiling usually reaches up thirty or forty metres, although single trees may push sixty metres skywards. Below the canopy other layers of smaller trees grow in the dim light that filters through. Diversity is the feature of these rainforests. Among the canopy trees of north Queensland more than 500 species have been identified and as many as ten per cent still await scientific description. The canopy trees must have leaves that can withstand heat from the sun and the drying effects of wind, but under them is a moist, warm world of almost constant temperature and high humidity. Leaves are large and soft, unlike the hard, leathery leaves of the dry forest country. Trunks tend to be slender, with thin bark so covered with algae, lichens and mosses that identification is difficult. Tropical rainforest trees also tend to be shallow-rooted and their rootlets feed in the surface soils. Buttress roots are particularly common in the figtrees and these plank-shaped structures often writhe over the ground. The giants of this genera of plants grow in rainforests. The best-known are the strangler figs which, though they can grow directly from the ground, usually begin life when a seed falls into the crown of a tall forest tree. The germinating seed pushes string-like roots towards the ground. Once the soil is reached the roots grow rapidly until they finally enmesh the host trunk. A well-known strangler is the curtain fig (below right) of the Atherton Tableland near Cairns. In this case the seed fell on a host tree with a sloping trunk. As a result the roots growing vertically downward lost contact with the trunk and formed a curtain.

The other common tree group of the tropics comprises the palms. The screw-palm (top right), a *Pandanus* species, grows along coasts and estuaries but also inland along the banks of rivers and in freshwater swamps. The Bangalow or piccabeen palm (left) has leaves arranged along a central axis giving it a feathery look. It is popular for garden planting but grows naturally from the south coast of New South Wales into the tropical rainforests of Queensland.

Over page: The Murchison River loop, Kalbarri National Park, Western Australia.

The history of European settlement in Australia spans only two hundred years, and recently much work has been done to preserve and restore historic buildings and other relics of the early days. Many of the most important buildings belong to the period when penal settlements existed in the Australian colonies to receive British convicts transported here to serve long sentences. Some of the most important relics of the convict days are preserved in Tasmania. In 1825 Maria Island (above), off Tasmania's south-east coast, was set aside for a penal settlement. The settlement was closed in 1832 but in 1843 a probation station was opened on the site. During the next seven years brick buildings were constructed by convict labour. Many of those with historical significance are now being restored. Left: Ruins of the castle-like Round Tower surmounting the guard-house and magazine at Port Arthur. Right: Ruins of the commandant's residence at the former convict settlement, Lynton, Western Australia.

The convict era in Australia was followed by the gold rushes of the 1850s. Many convicts who completed or escaped their servitude joined an influx of free settlers in the hunt for the gold which had been found in large quantities in south-eastern Australia. Victoria's main cities were virtually established by the boom years which followed the gold discoveries; the two most famous were at Ballarat and Bendigo in central Victoria. Both cities retain many reminders of their gold-mining days and at Ballarat a substantial open-air gold mining museum has been established at Sovereign Hill on the site of an old mine (left). Here tourists can take rides in horse-drawn vehicles, pan for gold, explore the mine and browse in historically-accurate reconstructions of shops and public buildings.

Right: Remains of the old water-wheel, Fenton Forest, Tasmania. Below: Historic stone mill and cottage under repair at Oatlands, Tasmania.

The once-common blacksmith's shop of Australia's colonial days is now long a thing of the past. A faithful recreation (left) is among the many displays of pioneer crafts at Victoria's Emu Bottom homestead near Sunbury. Re-enactments of pioneer life here are representative of the daily routines which were followed on the sheep station in the early days of the nineteenth century. The kitchen fire burned continuously through summer and winter, for there was no stove. Pots and pans were hung from hooks or chains or from the cooking crane. Meat could be cooked either on a spit or in a camp oven which was placed among the coals and could be used also for cakes and scones. Once or twice a week bread was made in the bread oven. Food was kept in zinc-wired safes and bulk supplies were stored in a special place in the roof. Washing was done in wooden buckets, and the kitchen duties also included making candles and soap, butter and cheese. In the stables (below), which are still used, the horses were housed, feed was stored and harness and riding gear were kept.

A CURREY O'NEIL BOOK
John Currey, O'Neil Publishers Pty Ltd
Melbourne Australia
© John Currey, O'Neil Pty Ltd
First published 1981
Set and designed in Australia
Printed and bound in Singapore
ISBN 0 85902 192 0

PHOTOGRAPHY

Australian Information Service: 12 (left, below).
John Brownlie: 1; 24 (top); 31; 32; 33; 39 (top).
Jocelyn Burt: 4; 12-13; 55 (below); 58 (top); 63.
John Carnemolla: 12 (top left, right); 19;
41 (below); 44; 58 (below).
Department of Science and Technology: 50;
51 (below).
Harry Frauca: 54.
Gary Lewis: 2; 14-15; 40; 60 (below).
F. G. Myers: 41 (above).
Fritz Prenzel: 6; 10; 25; 44-45; 60 (top).
Murray Price: 51 (top).
Robin Smith: 8-9; 11; 16; 17; 18; 20-21; 22-23;
26; 27; 28-29; 30; 34 (below); 35; 36-37; 38;
39 (below); 42-43; 46-47; 48; 52-53; 56-57; 59;
61; 62-63.
Ken Stepnell: 24 (below); 34 (top); 49; 55 (top).